Alone In My Thoughts

Vivek Raveendran

BookLeaf Publishing

India | USA | UK

Presentation by *BookLeaf Publishing*

Web: www.bookleafpub.com

E-mail: info@bookleafpub.com

ISBN: 9789363316492

First edition 2024

ACKNOWLEDGEMENTS

As I step foot for the first time into this world of writing, starry-eyed and hopeful, I must acknowledge the impact certain people have had in my life.

My parents and my sister, who have been a constant support for me all my life.

My friends, who have been there to help me at my worst moments, who I seek to celebrate with my best moments.

My teachers, for whom I might have been just another student but who were for me, guiding lights.

And my wife. I haven't been great at finding love in the past, but I guess it was because destiny had in mind a good ending.

My Rightful Place

A body lost, dry and drab,
A body tired, recovering from a stab,
Your smile, faint, unassuming, broke through,
Invigorated the body, and I looked up at you.

A soul deflated, directionless, broken,
A soul exhausted, longing to be woken,
Your voice broke the lull, like fresh bloom in
spring,
The soul got life as it listened to you sing.

My will, shattered, wobbly and weak,
My will, searching for focus to peak,
Your eyes met mine, a connection divine,
My will to live reborn, a journey where you are
mine.

A life uninteresting, colourless, bland,
An uneventful life, passing by like grains of
sand,
Your touch, so gentle, had me in an embrace,
And in your arms, I knew I was in my rightful
place.

A New Page Beckons

I sat alone, holding the book in my hand,
Unwilling to put it down, yet unable to
withstand,
Heavy, erratic, it told a whimsical tale,
It felt so large in scale, still so minute in detail.

A page I just finished, it took me time to grasp,
Twisting winding the path it took, I sat, unable
to unclasp,
Some verses delightful, some lines abject, yet all
making sense,
Words no more, I was living through them,
unable to sit on the fence.

I ended the page, short of breath; it took a lot out
of me,

The next page beckoned, without a pause, more
it wanted me to see,
Scared, anxious of what lay ahead, I turned the
page with care,
A part of me excited, a part living on a prayer.

I realised as the new page emerged, it was never
about free will,
The page will turn, come what may, handle it
with utmost skill,
You are the author, the page is blank, fill it up,
go for glory,
A new chapter, a new subplot, write your very
own story.

Persevere

Defeated, his spirit broken, he walked brooding,
Searching for relief, a hope, a light, a word
soothing,
At odds with the past, in conflict with the now,
An uncertain future he wanted to solve but
without an inkling how.

He'd kept trying, toiling away, but couldn't
seem to catch a break,
A cruel joke by life it seemed, a glimpse here, a
glimmer there, alas, but fake,
He waited, surely his luck will turn; in his
favour, the winds will sway,
A gentle gust kissed by, showing what he
missed, only to turn back away.

He'd wonder what he's doing wrong, how he
could set the stage right,
He longed for the time when he was happy,
content, peace within his sight,
Being nice became a curse for him, nice never
got him joy,
Nice is for the weak – be selfish, cunning tactics
you must employ.

His Teacher was calm, her face serene as the
pupil's rant ended,
He looked upon her with hopeful eyes, she knew
he wanted his heart mended,
She said one word is all there is, to believe, to
do, to mention here,
No matter how low, no matter how down, get
up, show up and Persevere.

Love

A hug, a kiss, a touch that you miss,
A smile, a peek, a gaze making you weak,
A playful wink, cheeks that go pink,
And you wonder if it's a dream – will it
disappear if you blink.

An unplanned date, who cares if the coffee
wasn't great,
That blush on a compliment, that listening
without judgement,
Conversations without a beginning,
conversations that don't seem to end,
And you wonder if your heart is finally on the
mend.

That holding of hands, like music of the bands,
A journey together in sight, a string to your kite,
A shoulder to lean on, a shoulder to stand on,
And you wonder if, for someone, you're finally
a priority, not a pawn.

Good times like morning sunshine, heavenly,
divine,
Then also came the storm, threatening to
deform,
That voice that made you swoon says we'll
dance together no matter what tune,
Stop wondering, you have your soulmate, you
are immune.

Take A Chance

A hint of indecision, a sliver of hesitation,
A bite of the tongue that holds back a
conversation,
A sense of fear, a feeling of unease,
A question almost uttered, cloaked in
trepidation.

And in your mind, a whirlwind of emotion,
What if the ship has sailed to another
destination?
A frown on the query, an untoward reaction,
What if it's ridiculed, trampled, shoved into
rejection.

But what scares you most is the assumption,
Of an answer that breaks you, shatters your
perception,
The hope that you held on to, a sapling that you
nurtured,
About to wither and dry, suffering an infarction.

But when on that precipice, ponder this my
friend,
What you never ask about is destined to end,
Go for it, take that shot, it only increases the
odds,
Do the best that you can, leave the rest up to the
Gods.

Yes, it would sting, some pain you will endure,
If what you wished is not scripted, if it's not
what you were hoping for,
Much worse though, my friend, is the constant
regret,
Of an ask never uttered, of a reply you never get.

Some call it closure, some would term it clarity,
Maybe unclear at present, but you need it for
your sanity,
Gather courage, take that leap, do not give
inhibitions a glance,
Be unfettered by the mind's misgivings, be
brave, take a chance.

The Wandering Traveller

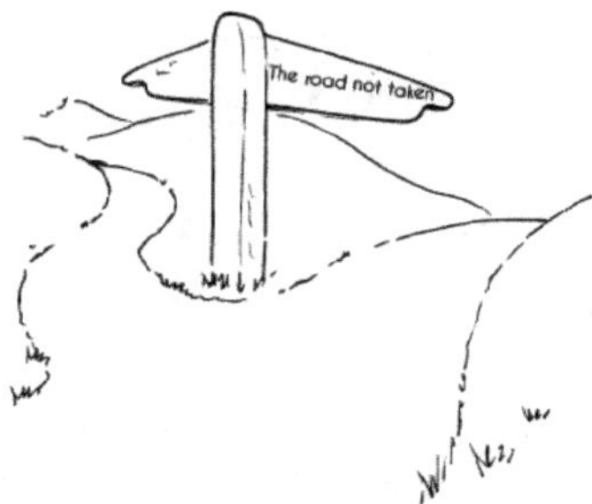

The wind swayed, whooshed and howled,
The darkness everywhere knew no bounds,
Yet he stood there, smiling, inviting them on,
For in all this chaos, he was home.

The new lands – virgin, unexplored – were his
companion,
For the night his abode, for the journey his
stallion,
The strangers he met were his family that night,
His mother, father, sister holding him tight.

The road he traversed was his wife,
Hugging him passionately, kissing him with life,
And when his spirit wavered, she sung out an
angelic set,
Keep going my love, she said, our story doesn't
end just yet.

He crossed mountains, forest and rivers galore,
Not once feeling he was lost or bored,
It was this that life was meant to be,
Not sitting behind a desk, wondering what all
one could see.

As he dipped his feet in the stream, he
reminisced,
Of all the time he lost, the chances he missed,
In pursuit of worldly pleasures, he had lost out
on the joy,
The sight of nature brought, the cold water his
toy.

As he headed back to the concrete jungle, he
heard,
The wind whistling again, serenading him like a
bird,
A smile broke his lips, he turned and ran,
Towards the wind, back to nature without a plan.

In all this chaos, he felt at home forever,
For he aspired to be no one but a wandering
traveller.

A Pause…

I take a pause today,
From the world outside, from the turmoil within,
A lot of noise numbing my senses,
Just detaching myself to be free from the din.

The mad rush of life sometimes takes over,
Halting the progress that you envisioned in your
journey,
It's ok to take a step back and reflect,
Whether you want to keep going this way and
end up on a gurney,

Take time to improve yourself, head out,
explore,

Learn something new, meet new people, try out
things you never knew existed,
Grow as a person, grow as a human,
You will never find this knowledge in the books
that teachers insisted.

The chaos of existence will inevitably call you
back,
And tell you to start running again, unless you
want to be left behind,
But today, I take a pause, from the world
outside, from the turmoil within,
A pause between sprints, for some peace to my
mind.

Hope

I stared at the vast emptiness that lay ahead,
Like barren land that hadn't been fed,
it struck me how the setting was a reminder so
poignant,
Of how we all wish a part of us was a
clairvoyant.

No one knows how that emptiness will be filled,
Will colours morph into a masterpiece or will
they be spilled,
If only there was a hint, a sign from above,
A message telling our fate, flown down by a
dove.

But the clouds won't part, the message won't
come,
Patience tested, resolve gauged, The One above
is mum,
The pain of the wait is dire, but still so alluring,
Even though the end might break me to a point
well past curing.

The lights fade out, darkness grows, I wonder if
it's the end,
A sunset preceding a rejuvenating sunrise or a
black hole around the bend,
A smell wafts through, tingling the senses anew,
I wonder how it will feel,
A fragrance to arouse, invigorate or a stench
that'll make me squeal.

So many thoughts pass through, and I open my
eyes,
The canvas is still empty, the emptiness still
there, I look up to the skies,
Why create something so beautiful, so beguiling,
but yet so cruel,
As the wait for the unknown kills us, forces an
internal duel.

Hearts will break, souls will shatter, as long as
this evil exists,

Oh yes, I call it evil, because that's the only term
that fits,
What else could you call something, enchanting
the human race,
To destroy ourselves so willingly, with an eager
smile on our face.

Heavenly yet savage, exquisite but still so vile,
Capable of tearing us apart effortlessly, our
bodies in a pile,
I wonder if mankind will ever find a way to
cope,
With this wretched thing, this thing that we call
HOPE.

Petrichor

The droplets fell down, like pearls from a broken necklace,
Valuable, each one of them, but meaning so much more together,
And with each kiss of the parched earth, they sang,
A song of yearning, of an urge to break down the tether.

To the lovers, it brought the memories of the beloved,
Of the kisses and the hugs, feelings no one else could explain,
To those broken in love, it brought sweet pain,
That longing of just holding hands once again.

To the one lost in the maze called life,
It brought a wave of nostalgia, a sense of respite,
For a moment, the inner kid voiced aloud,
Go out, get drenched, wash away all that eats
you every night.

To the city so lost, so hurt by the troubling times
it brought,
Hope and belief, to the stranded at sea, a sight of
the shore,
Hope that people will smile again, love again,
trust again,
Ah, the beauty of the rains, the magic of
Petrichor!

Life

It knocked me down; I suffered a pain unbeknownst,
Then picked me up, a guest I became to this gracious host,
I sat confused, how it could bring me joy yet put me in strife,
Its mysterious ways dawned on me – this strange thing called life.

Hope says it'll end up well; belief says it surely will,
life sees all but says nothing, never does it take counsel,
Every day a page you haven't read yet, every day an adventure unknown,
Every day a struggle, every day a joy, either a beggar or a seat on the throne.

And yet, no matter how unpredictable, it is the
only one we got,
Better make the most of it, better give it your
best shot,
So many things to be grateful for, so many
things to cherish,
Then why keep blaming yourself for every small
blemish.

A dream you held dear, which didn't bear fruit
and died,
Love you longed for but wasn't meant to be, for
which you cried,
Friendships that were supposed to last forever
but failed,
Opportunities that were there for the taking but
sailed.

So now I've learnt that it's us who must change,
Every breath a test, every day a chain of steps to
arrange,
No sorrow eternal, no happiness that will last,
No worries for the future, no baggage of the
past.

This turbulence taught me to welcome life with
an embrace,
To let it come rather than chase it, pining for joy
in every phase,

I'll still live fully, love deeply, still be honest
with myself every day,
Failure a lesson, success a blessing, what's
meant to be will come and stay.

The Call Of The Forest

An oasis in the desert of concrete,
A rare elixir in a city where toxins are replete,
I came for a stroll, and the calmness purified me,
As I walked deeper into the woods, it
surrounded and pacified me.

The forest shut out the madness outside,
inspiring me to do the same,
To portray calmness, even when the mind might
be playing a chaotic game,
Entropy is universal, it's inescapable, much like
death,
But let it not consume you, the forest said, be
alive with every breath.

Heartbreak

He stood there, waiting, bearing, bracing,
The winds too cold, too cruel, piercing,
Ripping into his innards, splicing them open,
The wails of his soul now dead, the courage
broken.

He wondered why they professed time heals,
He wondered if they saw how shattered his mind
feels,
From the constant barrage of attacks, all lethal,
Stabbed, lynched, shot, castrated in upheaval.

And every time before another shock,
Life would give a glimmer of hope, a tiny bit of
joy unlocked,
Like a pig for slaughter, fed well before the
strike,
The carcass then out on display, suspended on a
pike.

Why the blows again and again, he implored,
Why these continuing attacks, aren't you bored?
Just finish it off with one swift blow,
It should only take a second, please, nothing too
slow.

What was done, what crime was committed,
To warrant this phase – he asked – begging to be
acquitted,
All he wanted was a semblance of normal life,
A hand to hold, a friend to cherish, some sanity
without strife.

But he only gets a mocking laugh from above,
His destiny is such, a life without love,
And so he must live out this torture that's been
hurled,
An existence worse than Hell in this mortal
world.

The Light Within Us

A book in the corner, forgotten, withered, a little
torn,
Hidden in the shelf, it's gaze forlorn,
It seemed so familiar, so close to my soul,
For it was a journal from youth, where I penned
my life goal.

I brushed the dust off, opened the senile pages,
I read my dreams again, imprisoned in my
numerous cages,
This must have been divine, this intervention,
this pause,
Someone knew I was heading astray, adrift from
my cause.

Like a beacon, the words rang out, a ray of light
in a tunnel dark,
Egging me on to be righteous, pushing me to
leave a mark,
Challenges won't ever end in life, the pressure
will never cease,
Endure, withstand, defeat the evil, be good and
you'll find your peace.

If ever you find yourself in the dark, afraid,
uncertain, tense,
Remember the light within you, defog your
inner lens,
cut through the gloom, like a diamond from a
mine,
Chin up, ready for battle, it's your time to shine!

A Prayer

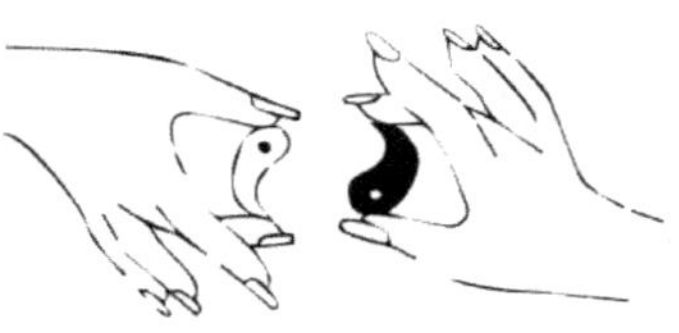

The soul, for so long quelled, seething under the
facade,
Of the smile, wide and full, disguising so well
the anguish within,
Engulfed by the cage abstract, stabbed by a
shard,
It yearns for the flight; it awaits its djinn.

So much that it wants to do, to say, to achieve, to
convey,
But trapped under life's mound of mundane
mediocrity,
It hopes it can soar, even if just for a day,
Away from this milieu, away from the hypocrisy.

How beautiful that day would be, ethereal for
sure, definitely idyllic,
A chance to show how life should be lived – like
a blessing,
Where eyes would talk and love would flow like
music,

Hearts would merge, happiness overflowed, the thought itself so refreshing.

It wanted to scream, from the edge of a cliff, so the whole world could hear,
A plea, heartfelt, to the machines of the world, passing off as mankind,
Hoping, as it lay chained, for someone to lend an ear,
Praying, still optimistic, someday true purpose they will find.

Is It Me Or Is It The World?

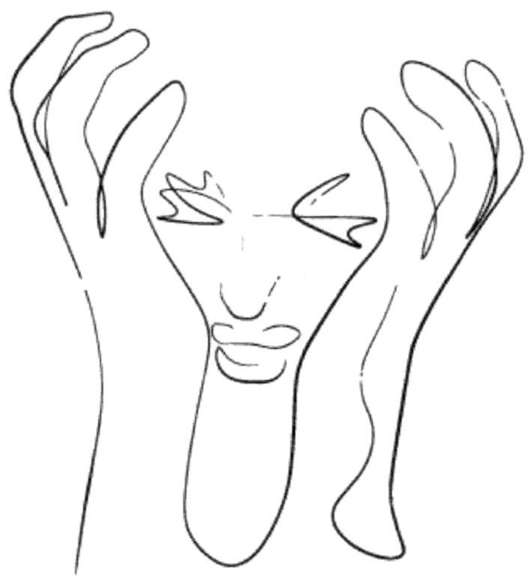

Every morning I rise from my slumber, trying to forget yesterday,
Hoping for a better today, a better tomorrow,
I cry out to the heavens, asking for forgiveness,
And a little relief from my sorrow.

I look to my side; there's no one with me,
I look above; the roof doesn't seem to be my home,
So I ask this to the Almighty above: Is it me or is it the world??
Why do I feel like an ever-gloomy gnome??

Of course, it is the world, it is cruel, it is callous,
it is unfair
It has denied me my happiness
It has left me alone, in a place unknown,
It has drained me of my freshness

I try my best to make it right, but it hits me back
It hits me so hard that I fall
It hurts, oh God, it hurts so bad,
It doesn't even let me stand up tall.

But how can the world be biased towards me??
I ain't the sole speck; there are billions more that
exist.
I see others happy, content and satisfied; how
does that happen??
How come their paths don't find an evil twist??

So I ask again, to the One above, is it me or is it
the world??
Why am I living in a cage?
Light dawns upon me, I can see clearly now
I see the face of the puppeteer on the stage

It is me, It was me, It was me all along,
I decide where my life is headed
No one else controls me, no one else can
manipulate,

Only I decide whether to fly or stay grounded

All I need to do is look inside,
Find a goal and go flat out,
The world might throw tantrums,
I don't care; in my mind, I have no doubt

So next time when your heart falters, loses hope
And asks you, is it me or is the world??
Shout out the answer, it is ME! ME! ME!
And your joys will be unfurled.

If Only

I walked along the countryside, alone, lost in its grandeur,
The scenery faded away though as my thoughts went on to her,
I tried my best not to go there, a road I had crashed on before,
But the mind rendered me helpless, for it had already flown over.

If only I could somehow erase the memories that simmered within,
If only I could go back and undo the events that added to the din,
If only I could pacify the heart to bury the pain and look ahead,
If only I could amputate the parasite, my peace on which it fed.

I still remember the day I met her, it was
business as usual,
She sat across me that day, looking elegant in
white,
No bells, no violins, no mistletoes, there wasn't
anything special,
Experience had told me that looks don't always
make it right.

But then we spoke, something to break the ice,
A cordial smile and small talk were to be the
beginning,
Of something that grew like a garden in full
bloom,
Through endless conversations late into the
evening.

The talks happened every day, never had it felt
so real,
Organic, natural and so easy, we could talk
without a handbrake,
We talked about our hopes, our pains and our
losses,
Our dreams, our worries, and the life stories
each wanted to make.

And at that moment, when the masks were off,
the souls laid bare,

I found her beautiful, and it wasn't about the
pretty face,
For the face will grow old, scars and wrinkles
abound,
It's the personality that shone with such radiance
in her case.

If Only (contd)

But it wasn't to last; one fine day the
conversation ended,
Without reason, without cause, a bolt from the
blue,
Like a man washed ashore by the waves, I was
stranded,
Without an inkling of whom to call and what to
do.

I wanted to ask what conspired for her to act this
way,
Hoping for some clarity, I put forward the
question,
She ignored, avoided, shirking eye contact,
acting fidgety,

Leaving me wondering why I was facing this
insurrection.

I wanted to be honest; I told her how I felt,
How pained I was by the silence, how hopeful I
was of a resolution,
But all I got were incomplete answers, failing to
clear the air,
Instead of clarity, all I got was more confusion.

How could it mean nothing, all the stories that
we shared?
How could something more than friendship turn
into an acquaintance?
How could a bond that was becoming warm die
out like a wet flame?
How could something pure and honest suddenly
become a grievance?

I was called many names, the names weren't
very nice,
It was a birthday gift that was nowhere close to
my imagination,
Weaknesses I admitted under trust were used as
weapons to defile me,
Wouldn't a simple no have sufficed? Why the
character assassination?

There was so much I wanted to do, so much to
say,
To show her my appreciation, to show her my
admiration,
To show her how much I was in constant
wonder,
Of her smile, her poise, her effervescence, her
disposition.

I wanted to tell her so much more, I wanted to
listen to her stories,
I wanted to sing a song just for her, as she
swayed gracefully to the tune,
Travelling, wandering off, waking up to
stunning views together,
Our lives intertwined, our journeys converged,
shining so bright like the full moon.

And then in a moment that felt just right, we
would come close
Our eyes meeting each other, finding love there,
which was so evident
I would kiss her, she would kiss back, like it was
the last chance we had
And in that moment we would know that it's a
decision we would never repent

I sometimes wish I could peep inside her heart

There were moments I almost messaged her as I
tried unlocking the maze
Was I the only one affected, did it all mean
nothing to her?
That beautiful month and the turmoil that
followed left me in a daze

If only I could get the answers to questions
strewn around
If only we could get back the connection we had
found
If only she would face me rather than hide
behind texts or a proxy
Only one knows the answer, even though it's
quite clear to see...

Stay There, My Child

Carefree, without a thought of the world,
Was so easy back then, when you were free as a
bird,
Stay there, my child, freeze up, don't grow,
If you age, all you will gain is a furrowed brow.

Life will hit you in the gut, punching a hole,
It'll pin you against a brick wall and suck out
your soul,
Every time you think that the worst has gone by,
There'll come another twist to bleed you dry.

That's what happens, the journey is relentless,
Want to know the details? Oh, the list is endless,
If it doesn't suit their stereotype, you will face
castigation,
Incessant, unabated, they'll force you into
submission.

The strength required to keep your mind from
going askew,
Will be too much for all, save a few,
You will be pushed out, for reasons unknown,
Shunted, shoved, tackled and thrown.

Try not to get attached, my child; it won't end
well,
Once life hits, you won't even be able to dwell,
So hear me, child, somehow find a way,
Keep this elixir of innocence close, and keep life
at bay.